HOLY CITIES

BENARES

Anita Ganeri

Dillon Press
New York

First American publication 1993 by
Dillon Press, Macmillan Publishing Company,
866 Third Avenue, New York, NY 10022

Macmillan Publishing Company is part of the
Maxwell Communication Group of Companies.

First published by Evans Brothers Limited,
2A Portman Mansions, Chiltern Street, London W1M 1LE

Printed in Hong Kong by Wing King Tong Co. Ltd.

10   9   8   7   6   5   4   3   2   1

ISBN 0-87518-573-8
Library of Congress Catalog Card Number 93-72036

ACKNOWLEDGMENTS

Editorial: Catherine Chambers and Jean Coppendale
Design: Monica Chia
Production: Peter Thompson

Maps: Jillian Luff of Bitmap Graphics

The author and publishers would like to thank:
Saviour Pirotta for his help in devising the Holy Cities
series.

Dr. Rupert Snell, Department of Indology and Modern
Languages and Literatures of South Asia at the School of
Oriental and African Studies for his help and advice with
the text.

Bipinchandra J. Mistry for all his help and advice and for the
use of his photographs.

For permission to reproduce copyright material the author
and publishers gratefully acknowledge the following:

Front cover: Main photograph—A scene on the
Dasaswamedh Ghat; inset left—Flower sellers; inset right—
Ganesha, the elephant god—Bipinchandra J. Mistry

Back cover: The sunken Shiv Temple—Bipinchandra J.
Mistry

Endpapers: Front—A ghat scene with Hindu temples
behind; Back—A Hindu boy receives a blessing from a
Brahmin priest at the shrine to Gang Mata—Bipinchandra J.
Mistry

Title page: Ganesha, the elephant god with his "vehicle" a
rat by his side—Bipinchandra J. Mistry

Contents page: Shiva and Parvati with the bull, Nandi in
the background—Ann and Bury Peerless

All the photographs in this book have been reproduced with
the permission of Bipinchandra J. Mistry, with the exception
of page 15 (bottom right) and page 32 (top), which have
been supplied by Ann and Bury Peerless.

Contents

The meanings of the words in **bold** can be found in the Key word boxes at the end of each chapter.

The city between two rivers

The city of Benares lies on the west bank of the Ganges River in the north Indian state of Uttar Pradesh. It is the holiest city of the Hindus. About 800,000 people live in Benares but millions of pilgrims flock there every year to bathe in the sacred waters of the Ganges and to worship at the city's thousands of temples and shrines.

Benares is a busy, lively city full of noise and hustle and bustle. The city stretches from Raj **Ghat** in the north to Asi Ghat in the south. Behind the ghats lies a maze of narrow alleyways, called *galis*. These are lined with houses, temples, and shrines. At stalls, people sell brass pots, copies of the holy books, and flower garlands, and many other things.

The name Benares is a variation of the name Varanasi, which is what some people call the city. It is a combination of the names of two small rivers, the Varana and the Asi, which flow into the Ganges. The city lies

Waiting on the riverfront with coals for making a fire

between the two. According to legend, the rivers were put there by the gods to guard the holy city. The city's oldest name is Kasi, which means "City of Light" and describes its special sacred quality.

Key word

ghat a landing step by the river or a place for cremating, or burning, the dead

Early-morning bathers on the ghats in Benares

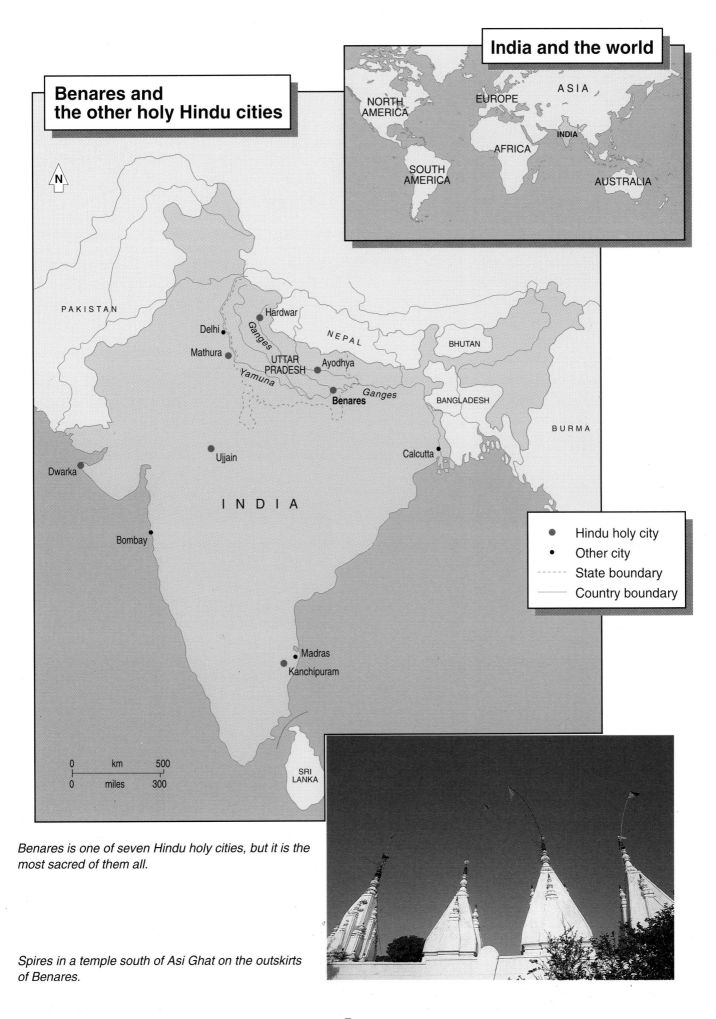

Benares and the other holy Hindu cities

N

PAKISTAN

Hardwar

Delhi

Ganges

NEPAL

BHUTAN

Mathura

UTTAR
PRADESH

Ayodhya

Yamuna

Ganges

Benares

BANGLADESH

BURMA

Ujjain

Calcutta

Dwarka

I N D I A

Bombay

Madras
Kanchipuram

SRI
LANKA

● Hindu holy city
● Other city
---- State boundary
— Country boundary

0   km   500
0   miles   300

India and the world

ASIA

NORTH
AMERICA

EUROPE

INDIA

AFRICA

SOUTH
AMERICA

AUSTRALIA

Benares is one of seven Hindu holy cities, but it is the most sacred of them all.

Spires in a temple south of Asi Ghat on the outskirts of Benares.

City of Light – City of Shiva

Benares is one of the most ancient cities in the world. Although no one knows exactly when the city was founded, it was already a thriving, well-established settlement by the time that Buddha, the founder of the Buddhist religion, visited it in the early 6th century **B.C.** At about the same time, the city had become the capital of the small kingdom of Kasi and was an important trading center. Kasi was one of 16 kingdoms established in north India by the Aryans. These were a people from northwest Asia who had invaded India in about 1500 B.C. They lived by farming and trading.

The kingdoms fought among themselves for control, and by the 5th century B.C., they had been reduced to four. These came under the supreme rule of Kasi's neighbor, the kingdom of Magadha. The name "Kasi" was now given to the city itself. Kasi grew and prospered. Between the 4th and 6th centuries **A.D.**, it became a respected center of Hindu learning and culture, attracting students from all over India. It continued to flourish over the next few centuries, under a series of Hindu rulers.

The invasion of Benares

In 1194, disaster struck. The city was seized by Muslim invaders and hundreds of temples and shrines were destroyed. In their

The Great Mosque of the Mughal emperor Aurangzeb

A statue of the Buddha in the Tibetan temple at Sarnath, the Buddhist holy city close to Benares

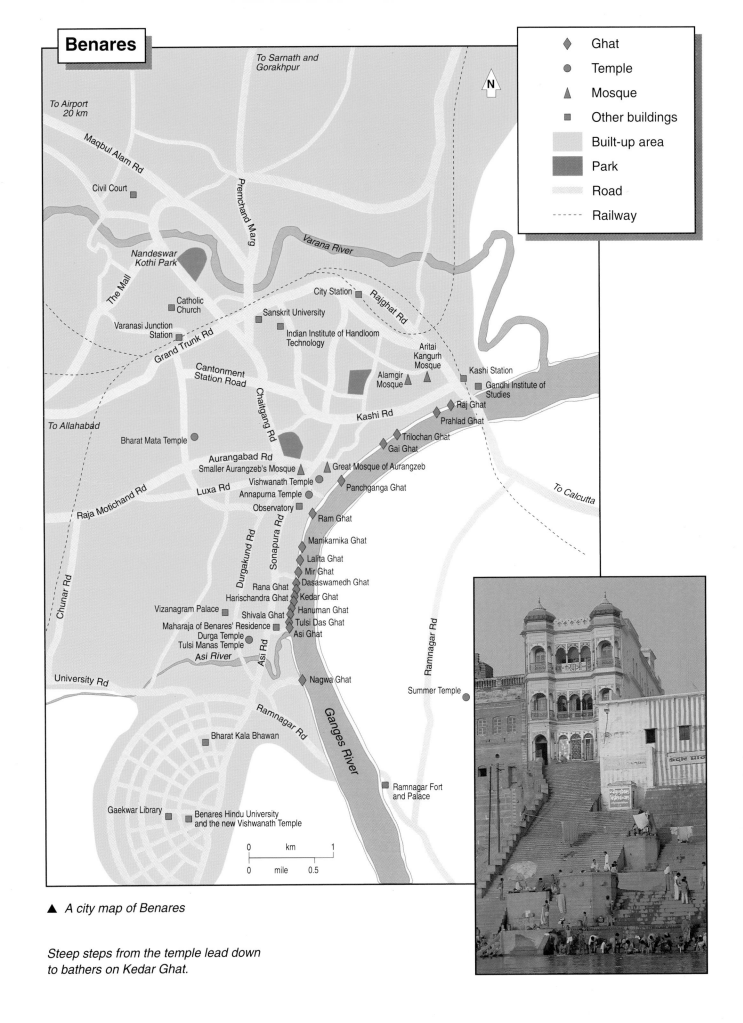

Benares

To Sarnath and Gorakhpur

N

	Ghat
	Temple
	Mosque
	Other buildings
	Built-up area
	Park
	Road
	Railway

To Airport 20 km

Maqbul Alam Rd

Civil Court

Premchand Marg

Varana River

Nandeswar Kothi Park

The Mall

Catholic Church

City Station

Rajghat Rd

Varanasi Junction Station

Grand Trunk Rd

Sanskrit University

Indian Institute of Handloom Technology

Aritai Kangurh Mosque

Kashi Station

Gandhi Institute of Studies

Cantonment Station Road

Alamgir Mosque

Raj Ghat

Prahlad Ghat

To Allahabad

Kashi Rd

Trilochan Ghat

Chaigang Rd

Gai Ghat

Bharat Mata Temple

Aurangabad Rd

Smaller Aurangzeb's Mosque

Great Mosque of Aurangzeb

Panchganga Ghat

Raja Motichand Rd

Vishwanath Temple

Luxa Rd

Annapurna Temple

Observatory

Ram Ghat

To Calcutta

Chunar Rd

Durgakund Rd

Sonapura Rd

Manikarnika Ghat

Lalita Ghat

Mir Ghat

Rana Ghat

Dasaswamedh Ghat

Harischandra Ghat

Kedar Ghat

Vizanagram Palace

Shivala Ghat

Hanuman Ghat

Maharaja of Benares' Residence

Tulsi Das Ghat

Durga Temple

Asi Ghat

Tulsi Manas Temple

Asi River

Asi Rd

University Rd

Nagwa Ghat

Ramnagar Rd

Summer Temple

Ramnagar Rd

Bharat Kala Bhawan

Ganges River

Ramnagar Fort and Palace

Gaekwar Library

Benares Hindu University and the new Vishwanath Temple

| 0 | km | 1 |
| 0 | mile | 0.5 |

▲ A city map of Benares

Steep steps from the temple lead down to bathers on Kedar Ghat.

The Muslims built many mosques over Hindu temples.

A painting of the great Hindu god Shiva

place, the Muslim rulers often built their own mosques (see page 25). But the great Mughal emperor Akbar (reigned 1556-1605) encouraged and helped Hindus to rebuild their temples. His grandson, Aurangzeb, was not so lenient. During his reign (1658-1707), many temples were destroyed once again.

By the late 18th century, the Mughal empire had fallen apart and most of India came under British rule. Large areas of Benares, including temples and ghats, were rebuilt with money donated by the Marathas, the Hindu rulers of the region around Bombay. Very few of the temples you can see in Benares today are over 200 years old, although they may stand on the sites of much more ancient buildings. India became an independent country in 1947.

A view over the sacred Ganges River from Asi Ghat

One of the many temples in Benares dedicated to the god Shiva

The position of Benares on the Ganges River makes it even more important. The Ganges River is sacred to Hindus. They believe that bathing in its water will wash away their sins. It is especially sacred and powerful at Benares. **Devout** Hindus try to visit Benares at least once in their lifetime to bathe in the river. It is even more favorable to die in the city and be **cremated** on the banks of the river. By doing this, a person achieves moksha.

The most holy city

Benares is one of seven sacred Hindu cities in India. The other six are Ayodhya, Mathura, Hardwar, Ujjain, Kanchipuram, and Dwarka. These are known in **Hindi** as *tirtha*, or "crossing places" from this world to moksha, which is **salvation** (see page 13). Benares is considered to be the holiest of the *tirthas*. It combines the goodness of all the other *tirthas* put together.

It is said to be the place chosen by Lord Shiva, one of the greatest of the Hindu gods, as his home on earth. He also chose it to stand at the center of the earth. According to Hindu tradition, when Shiva left his home on Mount Kailas in the Himalayas and married the goddess Parvati, he needed to find somewhere to live, and he chose Benares. Benares is known as the City of Shiva —there are hundreds of temples dedicated to Shiva all over the city.

Key words

B.C. the years before the birth of Jesus Christ

A.D. the years after Christ was born

Hindi the main language spoken in Benares and Uttar Pradesh as a whole

salvation being saved from sin and therefore becoming free

devout very religious

cremated burned to ashes

What's in a Name?

Hindus often call Shiva the destroyer because they believe that he periodically destroys the world so that he can rebuild it again.

Hindu beliefs

About 80 percent of India's population, some 675 million people, are Hindus. There are also many Hindus living abroad, in countries such as Britain, Malaysia, and the Gulf states. Hindus do not see their religion as separate from their daily lives. They see it much more as a way of life, affecting everything they do. In fact, the word Hinduism, meaning the Hindu religion, was invented by the British as late as the 19th century. Hindus simply call their way of life dharma, which means "a sense of duty."

Hinduism is different from religions such as Islam or Christianity. It has no founder figure, such as Jesus Christ, and no single holy book, such as the Christian Bible. A person cannot become a Hindu; he or she has to be born one. But it is an extremely practical and **flexible** religion, even if it is a little complicated. Hindus may worship one god, several gods, or none at all. They may worship at a grand temple or at a small **shrine** in their home.

How Hinduism began

Hinduism is one of the oldest living religions. It developed gradually, from the time of the

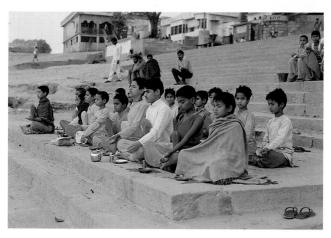

Brahmin children in early-morning prayer on Asi Ghat

Indus Valley civilization in northwest India in about 2500 B.C. Archaeologists have found many female statues, probably of a mother goddess, among the ruins of the Indus cities. There are also statues that may represent an early form of Shiva. The Indus civilization came to an end in about 1500 B.C., with the arrival of the Aryans. Their ideas mixed with those of the Indus people and marked the next stage of the Hindu religion. The Aryans' religious hymns, collected together as the *Rig-Veda*, are still among the holiest books of Hinduism (see page 39).

Puppets in the Tulsi Manas Temple act out scenes from one of the Hindu sacred texts, the Ramayana *(see page 40).*

श्री सीता स्वयंबर

A woman selling prayer beads and incense

The aims of Hinduism

Hindus believe in reincarnation. This means that you are reborn after you die. Reincarnation can happen many times, in a cycle of death and rebirth called samsara. The ultimate goal of a Hindu is to achieve moksha, or freedom from samsara. You can be reborn in many different forms, not necessarily in the same form as your previous life. If you have led a good life, you move closer to moksha. If you have acted badly in

There are hundreds of small roadside shrines all over Benares.

your previous life, you are reborn farther away from moksha. Your actions and deeds, together with their results, are known as karma.

The caste system

Since the time of the Aryans, Hindu society has traditionally been divided up into four classes, called castes. These were originally based on what type of work people did. The four castes are Brahmins (priests and teachers), Kshatriyas (soldiers and nobles), Vaisyas (traders and craftsmen), and Sudras (laborers and servants). A fifth group, the untouchables, were considered too lowly to be part of the caste system. They did the dirtiest, most menial tasks. Hindus are born into a particular caste and cannot change from one to another. But they can be reborn into a higher or lower caste, depending on their karma.

Key words

flexible easily changed; adaptable

shrine a holy place of worship, often with a sacred picture, ashes, or other holy objects

Gods and goddesses

A floating shop selling brass pots for pilgrims to carry Ganges water in and other items needed for worship

Hindus believe in a supreme being, called Brahman, who is found everywhere and in everything. Various **aspects** of Brahman are represented by the gods and goddesses. The three main gods are Brahma, Vishnu, and Shiva. But there are also millions of others.

Gods and goddesses are shown in many ways, as pictures and as statues. Hindus do not worship the statue itself, but the aspect of the god or goddess it represents. The gods are shown with symbols that identify their special qualities. They also have a special animal, called a vehicle, associated with them. There are pictures and **images** of the gods and goddesses everywhere in Benares. They are not just in the temples, but in stores, hotels, and even in taxis and **rickshaws**.

Brahma, the creator

Brahma has four faces for looking at all four corners of the earth. He rides on a goose and is shown as a priestly figure holding a rosary and a flask of holy water. His wife is the goddess of learning and arts, Saraswati. She rides on a white swan and carries a stringed musical instrument called a veena.

Vishnu, the preserver

Vishnu is shown sitting on the coils of a giant serpent. In his four arms, he holds a conch shell, a discus, a sword, and a trumpet as symbols of his great power and holiness. His vehicle is the half-man, half-eagle Garuda. His wife is the goddess of wealth, Lakshmi. From

The goddess Durga riding on her "vehicle," the tiger

You can buy statues of the gods from many wayside stalls.

The god Krishna, one of the forms taken by Vishnu on his visits to earth

time to time, Vishnu visits the earth to save it from evil. He has appeared nine times so far. On his seventh visit, he came as the hero Rama (see page 41). On his eighth visit, he appeared as the god Krishna. Both Rama and Krishna are worshiped throughout India.

Shiva, the destroyer

Shiva rides on a bull called Nandi. He carries a trident—a symbol of destruction. He has a third eye in the middle of his forehead that represents knowledge. The Ganges River flows through his hair (see page 28). His wife, the goddess Parvati, is usually beautiful and good, but also has a terrible side to her, as the goddess of battle, Durga. As Durga, she is shown with ten arms, each holding a weapon. She rides on a tiger.

Ganesha, the elephant god

The elephant-headed god, Ganesha, is the son of Shiva and Parvati, and is a very popular god of success and wisdom. He rides on a rat. Ganesha is also seen as a protector or guardian. You can see his image guarding

many of the doorways of temples and homes in Benares. There are also 56 images of Ganesha in and around the city, to guard and protect it from evil. According to legend, Ganesha got his elephant head after an argument with Shiva. Ganesha was guarding the door while Parvati bathed, and refused to let anyone, even Shiva, inside. Shiva was furious and cut off Ganesha's head. He later **repented** and gave Ganesha the head of the first animal he saw—an elephant.

The elephant-headed god, Ganesha

Key words

aspects forms or attitudes

image a likeness in the form of a painting or statue

rickshaws two-wheeled carriages pulled by a runner or a cyclist

repented showed sorrow for sins

A Welcome Visitor

Hindus believe that the tenth time Vishnu appears on earth it will be as a white-winged horse that will destroy all evil.

The Ganges and the ghats

If you take a boat trip along the river at Benares, you will not be able to miss the city's most famous and most visited feature. The riverfront has been carved into a series of long, often crumbling steps called ghats, which lead down into the sacred Ganges River. Pilgrims and residents of the city flock here every day to bathe and pray.

The holy Ganges

The Ganges is India's second longest river, rising in the Himalayas in the far north and flowing for about 1,550 miles until it reaches the Bay of Bengal, and the sea. For Hindus, the water of the Ganges is sacred all along its course. It washes away people's sins, allowing them to reach moksha.

The Ganges is heavily polluted with animal and human waste and the Indian government has set up a plan to clean up the river. Despite pollution, pilgrims have no hesitation about bathing in the Ganges, such is its power. You may see them scooping up handfuls of water and then pouring it back into the river as an offering to the gods. They

This sadhu is a follower of Shiva.

also carry water home in special brass pots. The Ganges is worshiped as the goddess Ganga as well. On page 28, you can read about how Ganga came to earth.

The ghats

The ghats stretch for about 4 miles along the riverfront at Benares, from Asi Ghat in the south to Raj Ghat in the north. There are

Stone lingams, the symbols of Shiva

about 100 sets of these long stone steps. Some have crumbled or subsided into the river. When the monsoon rains come in July, the river is three times its normal width and rises some 50 feet up the riverbank. Many of the ghats and their temples are submerged until the water goes down in September. Then they have to be dug out of the piles of mud and silt that the river has deposited.

Many of the ghats are crowded with bathers, priests, sadhus (holy men), beggars, people doing **yoga** exercises or **meditating**, and even sacred cows (see page 34). There are temples and shrines at every step,

A Brahmin reciting the Gayatri Mantra, sitting in the yoga position called the lotus

Children enjoying the holy waters of the Ganges River

including hundreds of lingams, the symbols of Shiva (see page 22). There is plenty of noise, too—prayers are chanted, hymns are sung, and temple bells are rung.

Dawn on the ghats

The best time to visit the ghats is at dawn, the most favorable time for people to bathe in the river. This is the time when they greet the sun as it rises. In legend, Shiva sent Surya, the sun-god, to Benares to be his ambassador there. Brahmin priests recite a morning prayer called the Gayatri Mantra:

Sun worshipers on Asi Ghat

"We meditate on the great glory of the divine Sun. May it inspire us."

The priests sit under large umbrellas on the ghat steps. They look after the bathers' needs, performing rituals for them, looking after their clothes, and preparing their horoscopes. In return, they are given token offerings of grain or money. In the past, the "token" sometimes took the form of the gift of a cow.

There are also sadhus, who bathe and pray along the ghats. They have given up their homes, worldly goods, and possessions to wander in search of spiritual salvation, relying on charity to live. Some are closely linked with a particular god. Followers of Vishnu wear three vertical lines of ash on their foreheads. Followers of Shiva wear three horizontal lines. These holy men may also carry tridents. The ash marks are called tilaks and are signs of devotion or blessing.

Sadhus use yoga exercises to help them concentrate their minds and control their bodies so that their souls can become one

Pilgrims and priests on Dasaswamedh Ghat

with Brahman and achieve moksha. There are many types of yoga. One of the best known is *hatha-yoga*, which consists of physical exercises and special breathing to relax the body and clear the mind. The exercises, or postures, are called asanas. One of the most important is the *padma* asana, or lotus posture. A lotus is a large white flower with open petals sacred to Hindus and Buddhists.

Along the ghats

Many of the stone ghats in Benares were built in the 18th century by the Marathas (see page 10). Others were built by wealthy princes and aristocrats, who still own them. These are some of the main ghats and the ways they are used:

Asi Ghat The Asi Ghat is one of the oldest and most important bathing ghats for

This dhobiwallah *(laundryman) is beating wet clothes in the river to get them clean. He will then lay them out on the steps of the ghat to dry.*

pilgrims. Unlike many of the other ghats, it has no steps. Instead, a slippery bank leads down the river.

Dhobi Ghat This is where the city's laundry is done. The *dhobiwallahs* (laundrymen) soak

These clay pots contain the ashes of Hindus who have been cremated. The ashes are ready for the priest to scatter on the Ganges River.

the clothes in the river, then slap them down on great wash slabs to get them clean. Then they spread them out in the sun to dry.

Pilgrims on Dasaswamedh Ghat buying religious souvenirs

Man Mandir Ghat This ghat was built in 1600 by Maharaja Man Singh of Amber in Rajasthan. His royal palace still stands on the ghat. In 1710, the palace was converted into an observatory by Maharaja Jai Singh of Jaipur. He was famous for being a great warrior and a great astronomer.

Dasaswamedh Ghat This is the most popular, and the most crowded, of all the ghats in Benares. Its name means ten (*das*), horse (*aswa*), sacrifice (*medh*). You can read more about this on page 29. It is considered one of the holiest ghats to bathe in. A main road leads from the city down to Dasaswamedh Ghat. The road is lined with beggars asking pilgrims for food and money. On the ghat itself, there is a temple to the goddess of smallpox, Shitala. Smallpox is a very dangerous disease.

Panchaganga Ghat Panchaganga Ghat is said to be the place where the five (*panch*) holy rivers meet—the Ganges, Saraswati, Yamuna, Kirana, and Dhutpapa. A magnificent Hindu temple that once stood on the ghat was destroyed by Emperor

These piles of wood on Manikarnika Ghat will be used for building funeral pyres.

Aurangzeb, who built a mosque on top of it. The ghat has many small shrines that open out onto the river. Some are used for meditation. Others contain Shiva lingams or sometimes images of gods and goddesses.

The burning ghats

Two of the ghats along the river are known as the "burning ghats." They are Harishchandra Ghat and Manikarnika Ghat. This is where people are cremated and their ashes scattered on the Ganges. People who die in Benares are thought to be extremely lucky and blessed. They are assured of moksha. Old and sick people often come to Benares especially to end their days in the city. There are also people who never leave Benares for fear that they might die outside the holy city. Other pilgrims bring the ashes of their dead relatives to scatter on the river.

A body is brought down from the city on a bamboo stretcher, covered in a red or white cloth. The dead person's family chants and prays as it follows the procession down to the ghat. Then the body is dipped into the Ganges and put on the funeral pyre. Burning the body is the way of offering it to Agni, the god of fire. The funeral pyre is made of logs of sweet-smelling sandalwood or neem

wood. It is lit by the eldest son, or a close relative, from an eternal flame that is always kept burning on the ghat. The ashes are later raked up and scattered on the river. After the cremation, there are 12 days of **rites** and **rituals** to ensure that the dead person's soul has a safe journey.

Harischandra Ghat is named after a king of ancient times. Despite his high **status**, he worked at the cremation grounds to prove his devotion to the god Brahma (see page 14).

A place of pilgrimage

People travel from all over India, by bus, train, and even on foot, to make pilgrimages to Benares. They visit the temples and bathe in the river. They may follow two special pilgrimage routes through the city and along the riverfront. Priests assist the pilgrims at every stage of their journey.

Panchakroshi The Panchakroshi pilgrimage follows a path around the outskirts of Benares. It starts at Manikarnika Ghat, follows the river to Asi Ghat, then runs in a large semicircle to Adi Keshava Ghat. Pilgrims take about five to six days to complete the 35-mile journey. They visit 108 holy shrines on the way.

Panchaganga Ghat—one of the five stops on the Panchatirthi pilgrimage

Panchatirthi This one-day pilgrimage leads along the ghats and the riverfront. Pilgrims have to stop and bathe at five (*panch*) holy crossing places (*tirtha*). They are, in their set order, Asi Ghat, Dasaswamedh Ghat, the point where the Varana River flows into the Ganges, Panchaganga Ghat, and, finally, Manikarnika Ghat. Then the pilgrims turn into the city to worship in the most important temples.

Key words

yoga exercise and deep thought, which lead to peace and calmness

meditating thinking deeply

rites religious ceremonies especially spoken or read from holy books

rituals performances of special rites

status position in society

The River of Life

The Ganges River is more than 1,500 miles, from it beginnings high in the Himalaya Mountains. Hindus believe that those who die in the Ganges will be carried away to paradise.

The temples of Benares

There are at least 1,500 temples in Benares and thousands more smaller shrines. There are temples along the riverfront, at the top of the ghats, and in and around the city itself. Most Hindu temples are dedicated to one particular god or goddess. Since this is the City of Shiva, most temples and shrines in Benares are dedicated to Lord Shiva. But for pilgrims, a trip to Benares provides the opportunity to visit other temples as well, each with its own gods and characteristics. Many of Benares's most ancient temples were destroyed by the Muslims (see page 8). Some of the present temples have been built very recently.

Shiva lingams

Wherever you go in Benares, you will see simple columns of stone, called lingams. These represent Shiva and are symbols of his power and presence. In temples dedicated to Shiva, lingams are the focus of people's worship, rather than an image of Shiva himself. In the

A Shiva lingam, covered in offerings

stalls around the temples in Benares, pilgrims can buy small lingams to take home with them or to wear around their necks.

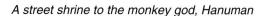

A street shrine to the monkey god, Hanuman

A Shiva temple that has partly sunk into the riverbed

The images of Rama and Sita inside a Shiva temple

The Golden Temple

The Golden Temple gets its name from its gold-covered spire. It is dedicated to Vishwanath, the name given to Shiva in his role as Lord of the Universe. This is the most sacred of all Benares's temples. It was built in 1776 by the rani (queen) of Indore and its golden spire was added in 1835. It stands near the site of the previous Vishwanath Temple, which was destroyed by Emperor Aurangzeb in 1669 (see page 10). In its place, he constructed the Jnana Vapi Mosque. Traces of the Vishwanath Temple can be seen near the mosque. Next to the Golden Temple is the Jnana Vapi (the well of knowledge). According to legend, this is where the Shiva lingam from the Vishwanath Temple was hidden for protection. Shiva is said to have dug the well himself with his trident.

Bharat Mata Temple

The Bharat Mata Temple is dedicated to Mother (*Mata*) Bharat (*India*). Instead of an image of a god or goddess, it contains a huge marble map of India with all the sacred places marked on it. The temple was opened by the peace-loving Indian leader Mahatma Gandhi.

The gleaming spires of the Golden Temple, which is dedicated to Shiva as Vishwanath, Lord of the Universe

Annapurna Temple

The goddess Annapurna is the wife of Shiva in his role as Vishwanath (Lord of the Universe) and so is an extremely important figure in Benares. She is seen as a kind and gracious goddess who feeds and cares for her followers. Annapurna Temple stands quite close to the Golden Temple. It was built in the 18th century, but the image of the goddess inside is less than 20 years old. Another shrine in the temple contains a solid gold

Worshipers at the Durga Temple, or Monkey Temple. It is stained red with ocher clay.

image of the goddess. This shrine is only open for three days a year, at the time of the great festival of Annapurna (see page 32).

Durga Temple

Durga Temple was built in the 18th century by a Bengali princess. It is often called the Monkey Temple because of the hundreds of monkeys that live in it. The temple is dedicated to Durga, the goddess of battle (see page 15). Two paintings of the goddess guard the entrance to the temple sanctuary, the most sacred part of the temple, which contains the image of the goddess. The image is a silver mask, covered in a red cloth.

The new Vishwanath Temple

This modern temple was built near the Benares Hindu University by the wealthy Birla family in the early part of this century. It is said to be a copy of the temple that Aurangzeb destroyed. Verses from the Hindu holy texts are inscribed on the walls of the temple.

The new Vishwanath Temple, built in the grounds of the Benares Hindu University. It is less than 100 years old.

The mosques of Benares

Although Benares is the holy city of the Hindus, a large number of Muslims still live in it. Two of Aurangzeb's 17th-century mosques are also still standing—the Jnana Vapi Mosque, or the Great Mosque of Aurangzeb, and the Mosque of Alamgir. Both were built on the site of Hindu temples. The remains of these temples can still be seen. The Jnana Vapi Mosque has **minarets** that tower some 230 feet above the Ganges River.

Tulsi Manas Temple

Tulsi Manas Temple is a modern temple, built in 1964 in honor of the great poet Tulsidas, who lived in Benares in the late 16th and early 17th centuries. His epic poem, *Ram Charit Manas*, is written in black marble on the white marble walls of the temple. *Ram Charit Manas* tells the story of the god Rama and his wife, Sita. It is based on the ancient sacred book the *Ramayana*. You can find out more about this and about Tulsidas, on page 41.

The Alamgir Mosque, built by Emperor Aurangzeb

Key word

minarets towers from which the call to prayer is made

The white marble Tulsi Manas Temple. It was built in 1964 on the site where the famous poet Tulsidas lived.

A visit to the temple

Garlands and sweets are given to the gods and goddesses as offerings during puja.

A Hindu temple is usually separated from the outside world by a wall. You enter through a gateway in the wall. The main shrine is in the temple courtyard. The shrine contains the image of the god or goddess that is special to the temple. This is the holiest part of the temple. There may also be other smaller shrines around it. The temple sometimes has a tank or well where worshipers can bathe before they worship. In the temple, people take off their shoes and women cover their heads as signs of respect.

Hindu temples are busy, bustling, lively, and very noisy places. The smell of **incense** is everywhere. People sing hymns and chant the names of the gods or passages from the holy books. Storytellers attract crowds of listeners. The temple is seen as the **deity's** home on earth. It is sacred but it is full of life as well.

When a Hindu visits a temple, it is not simply to pray but to have the darshan, or "sight," of the god or goddess. The worshipers bring offerings of Ganges water, fruit, sweets, and flower garlands for the deity. All of these things can be bought from the stalls lining the streets leading to the temple. The priest places the offerings in contact with the image of the deity, in order

A bowl of red paste, used for applying the tilak to a worshiper's forehead

may also walk around the shrine as a mark of **reverence**. This is called circumambulation. People walk in a clockwise direction so that they always keep their favorable right hand facing the deity. The left hand is considered unclean. This is why Hindus only eat with their right hands.

There is no obligation for Hindus to go to the temple, and there are different ways of worshiping in the different temples. Many perform daily puja, or worship, at home and only visit the temple occasionally. But the whole family is welcome in the temple, and children learn about the gods and goddesses by taking part in the puja and by listening to their parents and grandparents.

to bless them. Then he gives some back to the worshipers to **bestow** the god's grace on them. These offerings are known as *prasada*.

The priest also marks the worshipers' foreheads with a tilak of blessing (see page 18). A tray of small lamps, called *arati*, may be circled in front of the god. Worshipers

Offerings needed for puja. The trays at the back contain candies.

Key words

incense strong-smelling spices or wood

deity god or goddess

bestow offer as a gift

reverence deep respect

Legends and traditions

There are many legends about the gods and goddesses, and about places in Benares. These are just a few of them.

How the Ganges fell to earth

There are several legends explaining how the Ganges, the "River of Heaven," came to earth. An ancient king called Bhagiratha asked Brahma to let the Ganges fall from the sky to bring his 60,000 **ancestors** back to life. They had been turned to ashes by Vishnu thousands of years before (see page 14). But the king realized that the earth would shatter under the force of the falling water. So Shiva agreed to catch the river in his hair to break its fall. Then Bhagiratha led the Ganges from the Himalayas where it fell across the plains, bringing the king's ancestors back to life.

The lost earring

Above the steps of the Manikarnika Ghat, there is a sacred tank of water called the Manikarnika Well. According to legend, Vishnu dug the well with his discus and filled it with his sweat. Then he sat down by the well and meditated for 500,000 years. One day, he was visited by Shiva and Parvati (see page 11). Shiva was so pleased by Vishnu's devotion that he shook with delight and his jeweled earring fell into the well. This gave the ghat its name. The word *manikarnika* means "jewel of the earring."

Vishnu's footprints

Between the well and the steps of Manikarnika Ghat there is a large slab of stone. This is said to bear the footprints of Vishnu and to mark the spot where he meditated for so many years. Pilgrims always stop to worship here, sprinkling the footprints with sacred Ganges water and laying down offerings of flower garlands. A few very important people, such as the **maharajas** of Benares, are allowed to be cremated here.

A small boy praying in front of Shiva, who has earrings in both ears

The bull Nandi, Shiva's special animal. He sits close to the Manikarnika Well, which he guards. He is visited by many pilgrims.

sure that Divodasha would get the ceremony wrong, allowing Shiva to return. But the king made no mistakes at all. The sacrifice went smoothly and so Shiva was kept out of Benares.

Dasaswamedh Ghat, where the ten horse sacrifice is said to have taken place.

The ten horse sacrifice

The name of the Dasaswamedh Ghat comes from the Hindu words for "ten horse sacrifice" (see page 20). This refers to a very ancient tradition that was used to strengthen the power and position of a ruling king. Ten horses were allowed to wander freely. Wherever they wandered, this land could be claimed by the king as his own.

Benares was once ruled by a king named Divodasha. He had agreed to rule as long as the gods left the city and allowed him to get on with his task. But Shiva was determined to return. He sent Brahma to Benares to perform a ceremony called the ten horse sacrifice. Divodasha was told that he had to provide everything needed and assist Brahma with the ceremony. If Divodasha made a mistake, then Shiva could return to Benares. Shiva was

Key words

ancestors grandparents, great-grandparents, and so on

maharaja a great Indian prince

The Books of Knowledge

The earliest sources of Hindu mythology are the sacred books known as the Vedas. They were composed between 1200 and 600 B.C.

Festivals and celebrations

▲ Parents have no control over their children during Holi!
◀ These colored powders are mixed with water and splashed over people during Holi.

There are hundreds of Hindu festivals throughout the year, which for Hindus begins in March or April. Some are celebrated all over India; others are special to certain places, such as Benares. Of course, no one is expected to celebrate every festival—they would never have time for anything else! Pilgrims to Benares can buy special festival guides to help them plan their stay. There are also family celebrations during the year.

A festival of spring

In March or April, the lively festival of Holi marks the beginning of spring. On the night before Holi, people build bonfires and burn models of the witch Holika. In legend, she tried to kill her nephew, Prahlada, because he was a follower of Vishnu. But Holika was killed instead. The next morning, people celebrate by splashing one another with colored water and powders. It is wise to wear your oldest clothes! In the afternoon, people bathe in the Ganges. Then, in the evening, they visit relatives and friends with gifts of candy.

Getting drenched with colored water is an important part of the Holi festivities!

All dressed up, ready to visit friends and family on Holi evening

A festival of plays

The festival of Dusserah lasts for ten days in September. It is celebrated all over India, but in several different ways. In Benares, this is the time of the Ram Lila, a series of plays telling the story of Rama's life (see page 41). The plays are performed in many places including Ramnagar Fort, the home of the maharaja of Benares.

At the end of the play, Rama kills the demon king, Ravana. The actor playing Rama shoots a flaming arrow into a huge paper and bamboo model of Ravana. The model is full of firecrackers and explodes with a bang. The maharaja arrives at the final night's performance on an elephant's back.

On the day after Rama's victory, the Bharat Milap festival takes place in Benares. This marks the return of Rama to his home in Ayodhya and his reunion with his brother, Bharata, whom he has not seen for 14 years.

The lights of Diwali

Diwali is celebrated at the end of October or the beginning of November. It lasts for five days. Diwali means the "Festival of Lights" because there are lights and fireworks everywhere you go. The lights are intended to guide Rama home after his long exile (see page 41). Diwali is also dedicated to the goddess of fortune, Lakshmi. People leave their doors open so that Lakshmi can come inside. They keep a lamp shining to help her find her way. This is also the time when business people close their old account books and start new ones. In Benares, people float strings of oil lamps in little clay pots down the Ganges.

The arrival of the maharaja on his elephant during the Ram Lila festival.

The night of Mahashivaratri

The night of the full moon in the month of Phalguna is called Mahashivaratri, the Great Night of Shiva. This is one of the most important nights of the year in Benares, the City of Shiva. People sing hymns in praise of Shiva and visit the most important temples and lingams for darshan (see pages 22 and

A mountain of food

The day after Diwali is known as Annakuta, which means "mountain of food." This day is celebrated all over India, in honor of Krishna. But in Benares, it is also the time of a great festival to the goddess Annapurna (see page 24). At the Annapurna Temple, the shrine containing the golden image of the goddess is opened for darshan, and the temple is filled with food. This is offered to the goddess, then given out to people as *prasada* (see page 27).

The goddess of wealth and fortune, Lakshmi, is worshiped during Diwali.

26). On the day of Mahashivaratri, the whole family **fasts**—except for eating some candy or fruit.

Family celebrations

Hindus also have many ceremonies and celebrations to mark special events in their lives. When a baby is born, there is a ceremony to mark its arrival into the world. Ten days later, there is another ceremony at

On Mahashivaratri, priests perform puja to Shiva. The puja is taking place on Dasaswamedh Ghat.

The ghats are crowded with worshipers on the night of Mahashivaratri.

which the baby is given its name and its horoscope is made by a priest.

When boys belonging to the top three castes (Brahmin, Kshatriya, and Vaisya) reach the ages between nine and eleven, there is a very special ceremony. This is when a boy receives his "sacred thread" from the priest. The thread is looped over the boy's left shoulder and under his right arm. This marks the next stage in his life, when he begins to learn more about his religion.

A Hindu wedding is extremely important to a family. Most weddings are "arranged," which means that the bride and groom are chosen for each other by their families. A wedding lasts several days. Each day has its own rituals and ceremonies. In Benares, they include the bride and groom bathing in the Ganges River .

Key word

fast to stop eating food, or certain foods, for a particular time

Daily life in Benares

▲ *The bustling Dasaswamedh Road, leading down to the ghats*

The people of Benares are proud of living in their city. It is a bright, intriguing place that not only attracts pilgrims from all over India but is visited by thousands of tourists every year. It takes a little while to get used to the noise and crowds, but there are plenty of interesting things to see.

The streets of the city are packed with people, vehicles, rickshaws, and cows.

▼ *Sacred cows wander freely around Benares.*

Flower sellers with garlands of marigolds, roses, and jasmine

Weaving one of Benares's famous silk saris

A street stall where fresh vegetables are sold

Hindus consider cows to be sacred animals. They never harm or kill them and they never eat beef. All over India, it is quite normal to see cows sitting down in the middle of the street, blocking the traffic. Benares is no exception! In the heart of the city lies a maze of narrow alleyways. It would be easy to get lost in them. They are so narrow that you have to press up against a wall if a funeral procession passes by on its way to the burning ghats.

The main streets and the alleyways are lined with stalls and shops. Some sell the items needed for puja—garlands of flowers such as marigolds and jasmine, prayer beads, oil lamps, incense, prayer books, and religious trinkets. There are also stalls where fresh fruit and vegetables are sold.

Silk and saris

Since ancient times, Benares has been famous for its crafts. Two of the main craft industries today are sari making and carpet making. Benares is the center of carpet making in India, and most of the carpets are sold overseas. Hindu women traditionally get married in silk saris. If they can afford it, they wear silk saris made from Benares silk. These

▲ *Benares is an important center of classical Indian music.*

are famous for the gold or silver embroidery on them. This is called *zari* work. It is mostly produced by Muslim craftsmen who use very fine threads of metal. Buyers come to Benares from all over India to stock up with saris for their own shops.

Eating out in Benares

Some of the stalls lining the streets of Benares sell sizzling snacks, pan (see page 37), candy, and drinks. Most Hindus are vegetarians, especially in Benares and other holy places. A typical meal might consist of *dahl* (made of lentils), several spicy vegetable dishes, and rice or round, flat bread called chapatti. People eat with their right hands, often sitting on the floor.

Indian candies are very popular. They are usually made of milk or rice mixed with nuts. People give candies as presents on special occasions, such as weddings and festivals.

A typical meal consists of small dishes which contain a variety of sweet and spicy foods.

Pan is a mixture of lime paste, betel nut, and sometimes tobacco, wrapped up in a green betel leaf. People chew pan after a meal to help them digest their food. Benares is famous for its particular variety of pan. It is sold all over the city.

◄ Snacks made of flour and chick-peas. They are served with sour yogurt, and puffy balls of bread called poori.

▼ The triangular betel leaves used for wrapping pan. The leaves are chewy but edible.

Pan is sold all over Benares. Here you can see it ▼ being prepared.

Indian recipes

An Indian meal usually starts with a lot of tasty dishes in separate bowls and ends with fresh fruit. Try making this simple Indian side dish and drink for yourself. They are especially delicious on a hot summer day.

Roadside stalls sell all sorts of delicious snacks. This is a bowl of spicy potatoes. In Hindi, the word for potato is aloo. The red, pointed vegetables are hot chili peppers. Fresh coriander (a type of herb) is sprinkled over the top.

CUCUMBER RAITA

Ingredients
1 small cucumber, thinly sliced into strips
1 carton of plain, unsweetened yogurt
1 tablespoon of lemon juice
1 teaspoon of chopped mint
some black pepper
a tiny pinch of chili powder

What to do
Put the yogurt in a bowl and whisk it for two minutes with a fork. Add the other ingredients and mix well.

SWEET LASSI

Ingredients
$3/4$ cup plain, unsweetened yogurt
$3/4$ cup milk
$1^1/2$ cups water
6 crushed ice cubes
$1/2$ teaspoon of chopped mint
3 teaspoons of sugar
a few chopped almonds

What to do
1 Mix the yogurt, milk, water, and three ice cubes together. Ask an adult to do this for you in an electric blender, if possible.
2 Add the mint, sugar, and almonds and mix well. Serve with the other ice cubes.

Language and literature

The power of Sanskrit

Today, the main language spoken in Benares and all across north India is Hindi. India has another 13 official languages, including English, and hundreds of local **dialects**. But the language of ancient India was called Sanskrit. It was brought to India by the Aryans (see page 8).

The Hindu scriptures were originally written down in Sanskrit, although this was often hundreds of years after they had been composed. At first, they were passed on by word of mouth. Sanskrit was considered to be the sacred language of the gods and to have great power. It is a very exact, precise language. People believed that unless a prayer, for example, was spoken or pronounced absolutely correctly, it would have no effect.

Sanskrit later became the language of learning and scholars. Like Latin, it is still studied but rarely spoken except on special occasions. It is related to Latin and Greek. The Hindi language grew out of Sanskrit and became the language of the ordinary people rather than of the priests and scholars.

The sacred texts

Unlike the Christian Bible or the Muslim Koran, there is no single holy book in Hinduism. Hindus have many sacred texts, including the Vedas, the Upanishads, and the great **epic poems** of the *Ramayana* and the *Mahabharata*.

The Vedas The Vedas are the oldest of the Hindu sacred texts. They were used by the Aryans as long ago as 1500 B.C., although they were not written down until hundreds of years later. The Vedas consist of hymns, prayers, magic spells, **commentaries** on the hymns, instructions for meditation, and rules for performing sacrifices to the gods. They are concerned with the worship of the gods of nature, such as Indra, the god of thunder; Agni, the god of fire; and Surya, the sun-god. The oldest of the four Vedas is the *Rig-Veda*, a collection of 1,028 hymns.

The Upanishads The Upanishads date from about 800 B.C.. They concentrate on the inner

A Brahmin priest reciting passages from the Hindu holy books

world of people's souls, rather than the outer world of nature that was dealt with in the Vedas. They stress the power of knowledge and meditation, rather than sacrifices. Some 112 Upanishads have been written down in Sanskrit. They use parables and stories to teach their message. The name "Upanishad" comes from the words *upa,* which means "near," *ni,* which means "down," and *shad,* which means "sit." It refers to the way that pupils sat at their teachers' feet to listen to them.

Two epic poems

Two great epic poems are among the most important of the Hindu sacred texts. These are called the *Mahabharata* and the *Ramayana.* Hindu children hear the stories of these poems from the time they are very little.

The **Mahabharata** With some three million words, the *Mahabharata* is the longest poem ever composed. It tells the story of the war between two closely related families, the Pandavas and the Kauravas. They fight for control of the kingdom of Hastinapura, which the Pandavas family finally wins.

The most important and most popular part of the *Mahabharata* is called the *Bhagavad-Gita,* or "Song of the Lord." The setting for these verses is the battlefield, just before the battle begins. Arjuna, one of the Pandavas, is in his chariot. He is riding with his charioteer, the god Krishna. He tells Krishna that it feels very wrong to be fighting his own cousins. But Krishna replies that Arjuna must do his duty as a warrior, without thinking of how the end result might affect him. He persuades Arjuna that a person must not act selfishly. Instead, the way to salvation is through selfless action, devotion to duty, and knowledge.

The **Ramayana** The *Ramayana* is celebrated every year in Benares, and all over India,

These texts are taken from the Upanishads and can be found on the walls of the new Vishwanath Temple.

— 40 —

with the performance of the Ram Lila plays (see page 31). The *Ramayana* tells the story of Rama, the human form taken by Vishnu on one of his visits to earth. Rama is heir to the throne of the kingdom of Ayodhya, but he is robbed of this throne and sent into exile with his wife, Sita. Sita is kidnapped by Ravana, the demon king of Lanka. With the help of the monkey god, Hanuman, Rama rescues Sita and returns home to rule his kingdom wisely and fairly.

The *Ramayana* is thought to have been compiled by a wise man named Valmiki, in about 300 B.C.. A Hindi version of the poem was written by the poet Tulsidas in the 1570s while he was living in Benares. It is called the *Ram Charit Manas*, or the "Lake of the Deeds of Rama."

The monkey god, Hanuman, with Rama and Sita close to his heart!

A passage from the Ram Charit Manas, *engraved on the walls of the Tulsi Manas Temple*

The Stories of the Gods

According to mythology, the *Mahabharata* was written down by Ganesha, the elephant-headed god of wisdom. The stories were told to Ganesha by an ancient wise man named Vyasa. Like the *Ramayana*, the stories from the *Mahabharata* form the basis of Hindu art and drama.

A center of learning

Benares has been an important center for learning and knowledge for many centuries. It has attracted teachers and pupils from all over India and the world. They come to study Sanskrit and the Hindu scriptures and to continue the classical tradition of religious education for which Benares is famous.

Ashrams and monasteries

There are many ashrams at the tops of the ghats in Benares. An ashram is a mixture of a school, a university, and a monastery. Traditionally, it is a place where religious teachers, called gurus, and their followers live. Brahmin children are also allowed to attend the ashrams for their education. The ashrams and monasteries in Benares are important shelters for wandering holy men, called sannyasin.

Brahmin children come from all over India to study in Benares's schools and ashrams.

Sadhus studying the holy books in an ashram

Young Brahmin students

Sanskrit University

For hundreds of years, Benares has been the center of Sanskrit study in north India. The Sanskrit University was founded by the British in the early 19th century. It is famous for its rare Sanskrit manuscripts and wise scholars and priests. The British encouraged the building of the university because they needed a ready team of scholars to help them understand Hindu laws. The Indian government still goes to the university for advice.

The Benares Hindu University

The Benares Hindu University was founded by Pandit Madan Mohan Malaviya in 1916. He wanted to establish a modern university for the study of Hindu religion and culture, but there are also courses in medicine, engineering, and business studies. The university stands on a huge semicircle of land given by the maharaja of Benares. It is one of the biggest universities in Asia.

Writers and philosophers

During the 15th and 16th centuries, several great poets lived in Benares. The poet Kabir was born into a poor Muslim family. But he believed very strongly that all religions were equal and his work was influenced not only by Islam, but by Hinduism and Buddhism as well. People still sing songs written by Kabir.

Tulsidas (1543-1623) was a follower of Rama (see page 41). Very little is known of his life but it is thought that he was born in Ayodhya into a Brahmin family. However, his parents died when he was still quite young and he was forced to live by begging. He later decided to devote his whole life to Rama, so he moved to Benares, where he completed his famous Hindi version of Rama's life, the *Ram Charit Manas*. People believe that he was a great saint and wise man.

Founders and reformers

Two great teachers and **reformers** visited Benares in about 500 B.C.—the Buddha, who founded Buddhism, and Mahavira, the founder of the Jain religion.

The Buddha preached his first sermon in the Deer Park at Sarnath, about six miles away from Benares. A huge shrine called the Dhamekh Stupa is thought to stand on the

Pandit Madan Mohan Malaviya, the founder of the Benares Hindu University

spot where he taught. The Buddha urged people to follow a "Middle Path" of **moderation** and **compromise** that would lead to nirvana, or salvation. Sarnath became, and remains, a sacred site for Buddhists. Although its buildings now lie in ruins, it is a quiet, peaceful place to visit.

The Jain religion was founded at about the same time as Buddhism by a man called Mahavira. He was the last of the Jain teachers, known as Tirthankaras, or "finders of the path." Jains believe strongly in the value of all living things. They are strict vegetarians, and some devout Jains even cover their mouths so that they do not swallow insects accidentally. Their temples are extremely well looked after.

Over the centuries, many religions have been allowed to flourish in Benares. Nowadays, it is the Hindu religion that fills the city with its special atmosphere.

A Jain temple on Jain Ghat

Buddhist pilgrims praying in the Mulgandha Kuti-Wihar Temple in Sarnath

Images of the Tirthankaras inside a Jain temple

Key words

reformers   people who change ideas and ways of behaving

moderate   behavior or opinions that are not too extreme

compromise   a solution to a problem that satisfies everyone

Important events in Hinduism

The following are some important events with the dates on which they occurred:

B.C. BEFORE THE BIRTH OF CHRIST

2500 The Indus Valley civilization is at the height of its power

1500 The Aryans begin to arrive in India

1500–1000 The *Rig-Veda* is compiled; the caste system develops

800–400 The Upanishads are composed

500 The Buddha teaches at Sarnath and all over India; Jainism is founded by Mahavira

486 Death of the Buddha

300 B.C.– The *Mahabharata* and the

300 A.D. *Ramayana* are composed

268–231 Reign of King Ashoka

A.D. AFTER THE BIRTH OF CHRIST

100 Indian religious ideas begin to spread to Southeast Asia

320–475 The Gupta dynasty rules; Hindu culture and religion flourish

800 Shankaracharya, the Hindu philosopher teaches

1050 The Hindu philosopher Ramanuja teaches

From The Muslims begin to invade

1000 India and spread the Islamic religion

1469 Birth of Guru Nanak, founder of the Sikh religion

1500s Devotional worship of Rama and Krishna flourishes

1570s Tulsidas writes the *Ram Charit Manas*

1700s– The British and other European

1800s powers bring Christianity to India

1850– The rise of Hindu religious

1900s reform movements, such as the Arya Samaj, Brahmo Samaj, and the Ramakrishna Mission

1915 Mahatma Gandhi returns to India from South Africa to lead India's struggle for independence from British rule; he campaigns for religious tolerance

1947 India gains independence but is divided into largely Hindu India and mostly Muslim Pakistan

The Shiva Temple and Ashram on Kedar Ghat

Further Reading

Swani, Raghaveshananda. *Ramayana for Children.* Madras, India: Vedanta Press, 1991.

For younger readers

Ahsan, M. M. *Muslim Festivals.* Vero Beach, Fla.: Rourke, 1987.

Caldwell, John C. *India.* New York: Chelsea House, 1990.

Madhu, Bazaz Wangu. *Hinduism.* New York: Facts on File, 1991.

For older readers

Chakravarti, Sitansu S. *Hinduism: A Way of Life.* Jawahar Nagar, Delhi: Motilal 1991.

Miller, Barbara S. *Bhagavad Gita.* New York: Bantam Books, 1986.

Sherring, M. A. *Benares: The Sacred City of the Hindus.* Jawahar Nagar, Delhi: Motilal 1990.

Index